T0129373

Swan Songs

Poetry By

ALEXANDRA MOSS ZANNIS

Order this book online at www.trafford.com
or email orders@trafford.com

Most Trafford titles are also available at major online book retailers.

Cover design by Alexandra

Printed in the United States of America.

ISBN: 978-1-4907-4266-3 (sc)
ISBN: 978-1-4907-4265-6 (e)

Library of Congress Control Number: 2014913245

Trafford rev. 07/25/2014

 www.trafford.com

North America & international
toll-free: 1 888 232 4444 (USA & Canada)
fax: 812 355 4082

Contents

The Swan Song...1
Not Only Eagles Soar...2
The Death of a Deer...3
The Futile Journey...4
The Centurion...5
On Reaching One Hundred and Five................................6
Double Indemnity...7
The Festival of the Dead...8
Exhaling..9
The Face of Reality...10
The Invisible Man 11
The Innocents 12
The Wheat Field...13
To a Persian Poet..14
Fury...15
Black!...16
The Rape of Mother Russia 17
The Mesmerizers 18
Upon Reading Thomas Merton:..19
Eli, Eli,...20
Who Would Wash My Feet?..21
Requiem for a Dead Soldier..22
Chios Burning..23
Promises Never Kept 24
The Silenced Minority...25
The Donkey and the Elephant...26
The Squirrel and the Bird Feeder.......................................28
Perception 30
The Supplication 31
Conception 32
The Winter Wind...33
The Ghostly Parade 34
Winter's Tears 36
Winter's Dark Journey...37
Tin Men...38
Who's Steering the Ship? 39

The Transition 40
The Promise 41
Reality...42
Once Upon a Time 43
Gather Ye Rosebuds while Ye May.. 44
Reflected Images 45
Weariness... 46
The Tolling...47
The Silent Repentance 48
This I Tell You!...49
My Phoenix...50
What Is Love? 51
Plea to Morpheus 52
Full Circle 53
The Illegal 54
The Oath...55
To the Sun God 56
The House of Glass 57
A Letter to Spring 58
Braving Spring 59
Leaves 60
The Sucklings...61
The Tower of Silence 62
That Old Stainin' Tree...63
The Timing of the Snail 64
Limericks 67
Haiku..68
Beware of Your Prayers..69
In the Attic of My Mind 70
The Seduction of the Wind- 71
Ode To My Coffee Mug...72
My Little Poetry Book..73
At Sunset..74
Fame 75
My Father Wore Trojans 76
Ballad For Terri Winchell..77
Beware the Piper 78
Of What Consequence?...79

The Swan Song

One wonders how such a thing could happen:
the rape of Leda by a swan, whom the Greeks
claimed was Zeus in disguise. It's said he flew
into Leda's bed, forcing himself upon her,
his beak clamping the nape of her neck
subduing her, feathers fluttering against
her open thighs. Imagine such seduction!

Ah, the mythical aspirations of those gods
forcing their will upon lesser ones; but why
a swan? Would not a bull be more realistic
as he once raped Europa and carried her
upon his back to Crete? If a bull, Leda
would have birthed the golden calf
instead of hatching Helen of Troy.

And so the myths go on, with the gods
seducing, raping, committing havoc, posing
as birds and beasts for pleasure. But the lore
of swans was sacred to the ancient Greeks.
The muted swan was said to sing a dirge
as death approached: the sweetest of all birdsongs.

Not Only Eagles Soar

We look to the sky where not only Eagles soar.
We watch with dread as the Vulture circles above,
knowing his movements—wings outstretched,
no oscillation, the currents holding him aloft—
are the omen of death.

The great Albatross, hovering and swooping
majestically through the heaven,
became a curse in Coleridge's poem
"The Ancient Mariner"
when it was killed with a crossbow.

Rising on the thermals, the Osprey,
a symbol of heraldry as voiced by poets
and kings, glides the sky effortlessly
making their young fly to the sun,
dispatching those that failed this errant test.

Even the Owl, a majestic bird,
floats soundlessly as it swoops
down on unsuspecting prey.
A figure of wisdom, the Owl
lives in the silence of night.

And yet I still dream to be an Eagle
soaring through the ether, free
from all captivity of earth-bound gravity,
to feel the elation of ascending
into the heavens.

The Death of a Deer

Springing from out the cornfield
you leaped on to the road,
blind to the oncoming traffic,
your eyes focused on the other side.

You plunged into our car,
the force of speed pushing you
up and back, dashing you
on to the windshield twice:
thump! thump! Oh, dear God!

You were flung to the earth
stunned, lying helpless
but trying to escape. It was then
we saw your hind legs: broken,
mangled, hanging loose.

Involuntarily, I cried out,
my heart agonizing with your pain.
How many times you tried
to drag yourself to freedom,
how many times you crumpled
unable to rise and flee.

The end came
when the Trooper arrived
pistol in hand, aiming it
between your eyes he shot:
pow! pow! pow!
Your head fell in death.

I pray for you, innocent creature of God.
Man has stolen your habitat
forcing you to die in agony,
your herd never knowing
of your death. If they knew,
would they, like me,
shed tears of remorse?

3

The Futile Journey

Released from mother cloud
like eggs of a fish
being spurted into the water,
falling from heaven,
tumbling downward
by the pull of gravity,
coalescing with other droplets,
it formed into a raindrop
large enough to force its weight
down upon the earth.

Joining other raindrops,
it softly splashed into the river
merging with the billowing current,
becoming one with the whirl,
dancing, dipping, swirling
over stones and rocks,
bubbling with strength,
knowing no weakness
to deter its course.

Basking in youth,
never tiring from the force
of the raging river
but glorified with strength
and endurance, it competed
with the surging flow
forcing it into indiscernibility.

One day, the current slowed
edging it into a shallow,
motionless stream
smelling of dankness and rot.
Sinking to the murky riverbed,
it lay listless with face upturned
to the sky where rainless clouds wafted,
knowing only rain could bring revival,
knowing its journey was over.

The Centurion

Tall and stately, she is the epitome
of Byron's *"She walks in beauty,
like the night . . ."* Her life, often
bringing heartache, still retains
the purity of her soul, which shines
through her azure eyes like a beacon
of compassion and serenity.

The name Elizabeth suits her well,
meaning "daughter of God."
Perhaps her mother chose the name
knowing the beauty of that soul
laying in her womb, feeling
the tingle of every heartbeat vibrating
with love through her own body.

God has baptized you, Elizabeth,
from the holy well of His creation,
placing His hand upon your head,
filling your life with longevity
and compassion, knowing
you would do Him justice.

On Reaching One Hundred and Five

You've beaten the odds the world
placed against you. Jutting your chin
you defied the statistics on longevity,
daring statisticians to force you
into that common mold of life expectancy.

Surging forward, ignoring challenges
placed upon your body, you determinedly
wrenched those obstacles from your mind,
letting no barriers bar your path
to fulfilling the enjoyment of life.

Refusing to rest upon accomplishing
one hundred years, you demanded more,
priming your body to surge unrelentingly
into the unknown future: a warrior
flourishing his sword at the enemy.

Now at one hundred and five,
determination drives you onward
to outwit all statistics on longevity,
proving to the world there are no limits
when the love for life is insatiable.

Double Indemnity

You're not the lucky winner
In this speculative game;
It's those that pocket all the dough
Who'll be privy to the claim.

Could one of those recipients,
Who knew your coverage plan,
Be bold enough to form a scheme
To be that bogeyman?

If so, you'd better watch your back,
In case someone is stalking,
And never run across the street
When the walk sign says "no walking."

So listen up, you foolish man,
Why would you wish for double?
It's best you die upon your bed
Not tempting luck for trouble.

The Festival of the Dead

The Archangel Gabriel blew his horn
And all the dead arose
From out their graves and sepulchers
Where eons they'd deposed.

The horn of Gabriel again rang out,
Announcing loud and clear
To follow him triumphantly
For Heaven's Gate was near.

"Come forth," he cried, "you live again.
It's God who's set you free.
Shrug off the odious stench of death,
Come to Paradise with me."

What jubilation, what shouts of joy
Arose with the liberation
Of being pulled from out their graves
And saved by God's salvation.

Exhaling

The moment we enter this world, we inhale,
gasping breath into our lungs, sucking in
the alien atmosphere surrounding us,
announcing to the universe we've arrived.

How many inhalations are taken per second
of all human beings filling their bodies
with the gaseous chemical that courses
through their blood stream up to their brain?

Think of the exhalations from lungs
rotting with tobacco, narcotics, asthma
pouring into the air, polluting that which
we breathe into our respiratory organ.

Will humanity someday suck up all the oxygen
enveloping our planet, causing the corrosion
of nature, leaving us gasping our last breath
because of the proliferation of mankind?

And when we exhale the last breath from our bodies,
where does it go? Does it mix with the unsoiled
exhalations of new life, purifying the atmosphere,
restoring the planet's oxygen to its origin?

The Face of Reality

The face of reality is a satanic being
taunting our hidden conscious.

How can we look into those eyes
that are pinpoints of fire blazing

into our brain, searing our guilt
like an egg sizzling in a hot skillet?

We disavow that unacceptable face;
we pierce those eyes that attempt to strip

us of the impenetrable shield
we wove to deaden our sense of guilt!

How can we continue to live in deception
if we open the floodgates to reality?

The Invisible Man

He sits silently, his mind not functioning normally,
spinal cerebellar ataxia distorting his mobility,
his speech, slurring his words, making it difficult
to be understood, conversation minimal.

Most people are too impatient to decipher
what he is saying. He stares into space
isolated from society with loss of hearing,
unable to offer his innermost thoughts.

He needs assistance with kinetic tasks,
his brain unable to communicate
properly throughout his system,
making him dependent upon the help
of others in such functions.

He remains in his motorized chair,
maneuvering with the hand-held throttle,
roaming the house without purpose,
perhaps seeking to find the man
he once was to claim his lost identity.

He sits silently, unspeaking, slumped forward
in his chair, feigning sleep to avoid the sudden
embarrassing shift of eyes from passersby—
invisibility more acceptable than pity.

The Innocents

In 1999, two deranged students committed
the Columbine School massacre, killing twelve
students because of their anger for a few.
They gunned them down as they tried to hide
under tables in the cafeteria and library.
Twelve lives obliterated by mad men.

Five schoolgirls murdered in 2006
at the one-room West Nickel Mines
Amish School, in Lancaster County, PA,
by a thirty-two-year-old milk truck driver
who showed no signs of mental disturbance.
But the madness goes on . . .

At Virginia Polytechnic Institute in 2007,
a twenty-three-year-old student shot and killed
thirty-two classmates. The background
on his mental problems was never checked
by the school upon his entrance.
Thirty-two guileless lives destroyed.

In 2012, Adam Lanza smashed
through the door, forced himself
into the Sandy Hook Elementary School.
Holding three semi-automatic firearms,
he shot wildly killing without cause
twenty innocent tiny schoolchildren.

Little children, little children, no more to be embraced.
No more can mothers' arms encircle tiny waists.
No more can parents dream of watching you mature.
How unbearable seems the pain they must endure.

The Wheat Field

When I was young I was one with the waves
of grain bowing and bending in the wind,
flowing in the ripening yellow current
toward its destination of mortality.

I knew each stem of wheat that sprung
from the earth burgeoning and ripening,
each seedling a familiar source of life
radiating with the promise of maturity.

Some were the soft white stalks: sweet,
tender, pliable, striving always to please,
while others were the hard red winter seeds,
strong and sturdy, growing with determination.

As I aged and observed the familial scene
around me, the harvested stalks standing
upright in sheaves, their purpose of existence
complete, I understood the cycle of life.

Now I am old, a stalk of wheat that soon
will be immersed into the soil to nurture
the future harvests in this continuing story
of the beauty of the flowing field of wheat.

To a Persian Poet

Gazing upon the tree I named
in your memory, I envision you,
*"a book of verses underneath
the bough . . .,"* reciting softly
impassioned poems, your beloved
beside you, a jug of wine quenching
your thirst, a loaf of bread satisfying
hunger, your voice trembling with desire:
"ah, wilderness, were paradise enow!"

It is you beneath that tree,
dear poet, symbolizing the love
etched in your poetry, cooling
your fervent heart with its shade
as you inscribe each word
with *"moving finger . . ."*
I sit beneath its boughs
yet cannot pen a single line
that brings contentment to my heart.

Fury

Coming from the West, black clouds
raced across sullen sky:
iron tanks pursuing an enemy
unable to stand its ground,
tearing through the ranks,
scattering cumuli
as if they were bagatelle.

Then winds howling with fury
tore across the land impervious
of its deliberate devastation,
bending tree limbs to the ground,
forcing them to shudder in fear:
sinners kneeling before Christ.

Lightning ignited the sky,
a display of fractious fireworks,
pushing open distended flood gates,
spewing out watery wrath
upon arid soil as if to drown
whatever inhabited the earth.

Racing across the sky,
searching for other victims,
the storm passed as quickly as it came,
restoring heaven to tranquility,
night-tinted clouds separating
to expose to water-drenched land
the brilliance of a promising moon.

BLACK!
(The shooting death of Trayvon Martin in 2012)

Watch your step, *Black Boy*,
you're oversteppin' your bounds!
Hooded, black of night, cell phone in hand:
guilty!

What would you do if you were stalked?
Flee or fend your basic rights?

He turned to ward off a stalker
carrying an unknown object:
justifiable right to defend,
but killed for his decision.

The murderer declared not guilty
by a jury of six whites.
Who will know the truth?

I once saw a black man with skin
so black it shone midnight blue.
Drawn as by a magnet I spoke:
"What beautiful skin."
He looked at me unsmiling, defiant.

A white woman overcoming prejudice,
but he didn't say "Watch your step, *Honkie*,
you're oversteppin' your bounds!"

The Rape of Mother Russia
(1999 Resurgence of Communism)

You've been raped by your sons again!
They've clamped their calloused hands
over your mouth to stop your screams
as they thrust their bloody swords
into your throbbing body.

For one moment in time, you thought
yourself freed from their incest,
but they've returned with a lust
that dares the world to free you
from their stranglehold.

Will you again, Dear Mother,
bring forth another generation
of Communistic vipers
that will slither lawlessly
across your blood-infested land?

The Mesmerizers

I

"You must be reborn!" shouts the Jehovah witness
as he waves his magazine in the faces of passers-by.
        "You must be reborn
        through the word of God,
for only Truth can save your soul from Hell!"

II

A bedraggled radical convert, flourishing his Bible
in his up-stretched hands, paces the street shouting,
        "Save your sinful souls
        before it's too late!
The end is near! Christ is coming to condemn all sinners!"

III

The shaved Krishnas, wrapped in their orange shifts,
march down the avenue banging their tambourines:
        "It's only through love
        and divine love alone
that will bring you happiness and give you eternal life."

IV

The atheist absorbs each alarmist in his mind,
wondering what all the screaming and fury is about.
        "What a fool's paradise
        from these mouthing mesmerizers.
There's nothing but dust, dirt, and worms to devour our flesh!"

Upon Reading Thomas Merton:

"To be grateful is to recognize the love of
God in everything He has given us—and He
has given us everything. Every breath we
draw is a gift of His love."

O, Thomas, how can you believe such words
when you look into the face of a starving man?
How can you fold your hands in gratitude
when you see a helpless child barbarically beaten
or murdered by a degenerate parent?

Where is God's love when such innocence
is willfully destroyed by satanic men
who supposedly are created in the sublime
image of God and formed in His love?

Thomas, Thomas, answer me this if you can:
Where is God to protect that starving man?
Where is God to save that innocent child?
Where is God to restore our trust in love?

Eli, Eli,

"My God, my God, why have you forsaken me?"
Christ cried out as he hung nailed to the cross.
What pain, what agonizing pain
He must have suffered to have those words
forced from his vinegar-parched lips.

In Gethsemane, he prayed to have that cup
of anguish taken from him yet knowing
not His will but God's be done. He understood
the path He chose could not be changed,
even at this hour fearing the pain He must suffer.

And our soldiers who lay dying on the battlefield
must have cried out in despair to their God
to remove that cup of bitterness, "My God,
why have you forsaken me? Save me from this agony."
"Eli, Eli, lama sabachthani?"

Each of us in our hour of despair cries out
for this vessel to be struck from our lips.
Will we forsake God if we must drink it,
or will we quaff its bitterness with acceptance?
"Eli, Eli, lama sabachthani?"

Who Would Wash My Feet?

Jesus knelt to wash the feet
of His apostles, displaying
abasement, humbling himself
before them, reminding them
do unto others
as I have done unto you.

Pope Francis, at Casal del Marmo,
washed the feet of prisoners,
drying and kissing
those sinful extremities,
reminding the world
the teachings of Christ.

Once I washed the feet
of my mother-in-law
when she was old, unable
to bend, trimming her
talon-like nails, a job
my husband refused.

The sins of the world cling
to my feet, weighing them down
like concrete hung round the neck
of a Mafia dissenter tossed
into a river unable to surface.
Who would wash my feet?

Requiem for a Dead Soldier

Composed in D-flat minor, the black keys
sound the sorrow of death as heavy fingers
press down upon them. It is a dirge
lamenting this meaningless waste of life.

The music swells from pianissimo
to forte, as if trying to force the air
from the mourners' lungs
who sit transfixed in the pews.

The requiem strives to waken the soldier
with its sonorous thunder, attempting
to pry open the coffin's lid, freeing the corpse
lying disfigured in its imprisonment.

But the valiant hero cannot be released
from his futile death. No harmonics exist
to free the soul from the wages of war.
As if atoning for its violent outburst,

the music softens with the quiescence
of strings, quelling the flow of tears,
lullabying the fallen hero into a sleep
of eternal peace where he wars no more.

Chios Burning
(August 18, 2012)

It rages out of control consuming cypress,
mastic, and olive trees, destroying
the beauty of the hillsides and mountains
begging for verdant pigmentation
to cover their rocky crevices long past
ripped open by devastating earthquakes.

This ancient island is birthplace to Homer
and Hippocrates, the great mathematician;
from where Columbus took maritime maps
assisting him in his journey to America;
Lord Byron in literature and Eugene Delacroix
in paintings depicted the 1822 Ottoman massacre

that killed thousands Chians by butchering,
starving, torturing, raping, deporting
or enslaving, and then torching
the island to ruin. The burning of Chios
rages on today. Is it a continuing cycle?

Is the god Orion still seeking revenge
for his brutal treatment by Dionyssus's son,
then king of Chios, who blinded him
and threw him to the island's coast?
Perhaps from his celestial heaven he called
Hephaestus to cast his torch upon the land.

Promises Never Kept

"The wages of sin are death!"—also
the wages of virtue. We all must die,
even the godly who staunchly declare
there is eternal life after death.

Still, it is the hope of the virtuous
they will ascend that glorious ladder,
enter the pearly gates of heaven,
and be ushered into infinite life

aspiring rejuvenation of their earthly
bodies, floating on heavenly clouds,
plucking imaginary harps with adroit fingers,
weightless in their ethereal forms,
and devouring celestial ambrosia.

"Are there more things in heaven and earth,
Horatio, than the spirit can comprehend,
visions which are shielded from our eyes?"
I will return to tell you after I die.

The Silenced Minority

We're here, in the back of the room,
trying to raise our voices above
the roaring lobbyists, bureaucrats,
radical conservatives, inflexible
in their control over the masses.

Why don't they let us speak?
Why do they trample us into silence,
stuffing their extremist dictates
down our throats, wishing instead
to dislodge our vocal chords?

There is such silence among us,
we who believe in moderation.
Why are we afraid to raise our voices
against the belligerent strength
of those who covet control?

Are we the muted minority, too few
to form a strategy of strength,
too afraid to fight the autocratic power
that wills our suppression, striving
to trample us underfoot?

We must raise our voices. We must
scream above the oppressors;
but they will not let us speak,
for we are the strangled entreaters
pleading our right for democracy.

The Donkey and the Elephant

The donkey and the elephant strained at the starting line.
Said the elephant to the donkey, "I'm gonna win this time!"
The donkey raised his ears and, with a nasal snort,
Looked at his lumbering rival and gave him this retort:

"You'll never win, you lummox, your trunk will trip you up.
Before you reach the finish line, you'll land on your big rump."
"Listen, you old jackass," the mammoth shouted back.
"If I raise my tail and let it rip, you'll be blown off the track."

"But when I get ahead of you," said the ass in heated voice,
"I'll kick you here to kingdom come, and then you'll have no choice."
Now the elephant looked closely at this blustering pipsqueak.
He raised his snout and, with a blast, let out a roaring shriek,

"Look at you, you jackass, you barely reach my knees.
So where you gonna kick me to land me in the trees?"
Now the burro thought this over and with a smirky smile
Said, "I'll kick you in your bony knees that'll set you back a mile."

"So kick away with all your strength, you blue-ass jackanapes,
You're not the giant that you think, you don't have what it takes."
"You'll feel my strength before we're through, you red-necked bureaucrat.
You'll wish that you had never met a blue-nosed democrat!"

"Blue-nosed is what you call yourself, you hypercritic liberal?
Besides a flagitious leftist, you're an outright fibber-all."
The donkey thought upon those words, his anger growing worse.
"You'll eat those words, you right-wing thug, I'll cast on you a curse!"

Their anger grew so violent they thought their hearts would burst.
What good was all this diatribe when their lives were so coerced?
Then slowly did they quiet down and thought upon their plight.
Since they were the only party planks, there should be three to fight.

What better way to settle things than to form a third platform?
For then they'd have another prey on which they could barnstorm.
They thought and thought about a choice, as much as rivals can,
But a donkey and an elephant they aren't bipartisan.

The donkey said, "I've got a thought, let's pick a kangaroo.
As an idiotic jumping fool, that paradox should do."
The elephant just raised his trunk (that's where his brain was placed)
And shook it hard to clear his mind before he spoke in haste.

"I think it's wise if we surmise that a kangaroo's a name
That doesn't fit a twit on whom we want to place all blame.
How about a tired nag who's too old to win a race?
She'd give no competition, and we'd end up at first base."

The donkey opened up his mouth, baring all his teeth and gums.
He brayed so loud the elephant thought his hearing would go numb.
"What's wrong with you, you silly ass, for laughing at my thought?"
"I think it's great." The donkey laughed. "I'm really not distraught."

They both were very happy with this third party they had named
And hoped if anything went wrong, the old nag would be blamed.
But when the next election came, they really took a beating,
As the old horse had no candidate and the voters caught them cheating.

So the donkey and the elephant remain this very day,
Trying to outwit the other in every illicit way.
Now be aware, dear citizen, when you go to cast your vote,
There ain't no nag put on the chart to make them smirk and gloat.

The Squirrel and the Bird Feeder

I watched as he crept along the common,
traveling alone, a gray spot
upon the white snow, stopping
to lift his body upon his haunches,
turning his head side to side
like a surveillance detector,
then scampering across the white terrain
to find security before braving
to stop to peer around again.

Seeing no danger, he sped across the walk
skidding to a halt under the bird feeder.
Digging through the snow to find
savory seeds to fill his empty belly
and finding none, he attempted to climb
the iron pole up to the box.
Sliding back to the ground,
he tried again and with hungry
determination clawed to the top,
peering down at the food.

There it was, just within his clasp,
the container filled with all those seeds
swinging from the force of the wind.
But how to reach it? How to feast
upon that enticing banquet
that seemed out of his grasp?
To leap down was dangerous,
with the wind twisting and turning
the feeder in miscalculated circles.

But he was a resolute squirrel,
his mind working wonders
and hungry enough to take chances.
Clinging to the cord that secured
the feeder to the shepherd's hook,
he wound his way down to its roof,
gripping his claws into the wood.
Determinedly, he circled the top
until he discovered he could bend,
clamped his claws into the bottom tray
and grabbed the seeds with one paw.

The ingeniousness of animals!
He stayed for one hour,
fulfilling his hunger with food
for the birds, defying gravity.

Perception

What images come into our dreams!
What visions are hidden deep inside
our subconscious; memories we cannot
understand or even recall existed.

Why would I dream of this old man,
fine white hair like silk threads
covering his head; a body that life
was eating upon pound by pound,

until it was nothing but flesh
stretched across his brittle bones,
just enough to give him the appearance
of still among the human race.

There were two chairs facing forward,
he sat on my left as yet unspeaking.
I sat next to him not touching
but close enough to sense his presence.

Then without facing me, I heard him speak
in a soft trembling voice: "I am so cold,
please help to warm me." I did not recognize
this man, and yet I leaned against him,

placing my right hand on his osseous knee,
my left arm encircling those gaunt shoulders,
hoping the heat from my body would seep
into the pores of his benumbed flesh.

Who was this man to whom I was giving
my body's warmth? Why had he come
in my dreams so beseechingly asking
to be refueled with the calidity of my blood?

Was he a love of long ago, reappearing
to steal from me the heat of my body?
This I know, when love walks away
it takes with it the flame from our souls.

The Supplication

If there is life after death, I would crave
neither heaven nor hell. I would want
to return as a seedling in the earth,
growing tall and strong into a tree,
peering imperially over the land,
as Zeus gazing down over his empire.

With roots boring deep into the earth,
the juices of life flowing forcefully
through my body, I would withstand
the horrific forces of nature, living
for centuries like the giant oak,
stately, patiently, giving of myself.

I would provide a haven to wing-weary birds
tired from their transitory flights,
stretching forth my arms to offer them
security to bring forth new life to fill
the sky and earth with their songs.

I could ask for nothing more majestic
if there is an afterlife, I would say to all,
*"Come unto me, all who are weary and
heavy-laden, and I will give you rest,"*
beneath the shadows of my flowering limbs.

Conception

Conceived in the womb of the frontal lobe,
planted there by the seeds of inspiration
and concentration, nurtured by the placenta
of the thought process, it begins to form
into a fetus of words, expanding in size,
developing slowly into a conscious entity.

Upon reaching questioning form, it forces
itself from that protective chamber, and tearing
away from the umbilical cord, opens its mouth
pouring out unperfected words, making
the poet develop them into visual maturity,
laboring day after day to perfect them.

Slowly it grows, slowly it begins to form
into a product of beauty with each carefully
chosen word giving perfection and strength
until it blooms like a flowering cactus into a work
of acceptance, filling the poet with satisfaction,
knowing the birth was worth all the pain.

The Winter Wind

Do you hear it?
It's bearing down from the north,
bending the barren branches
of the bark-shrouded limbs,
making them tremble with fear,
knowing they are helpless
to resist its force.

Soon frigid sheets of snow
will push in behind it,
paralyzing the trees' roots
with its powerful pounding
until they are strangled,
lying listless and airless
beneath the weight.

Listen to the winter wind
howling and screaming out
its vengeance upon the earth,
defying any resistance
to its polarizing purge
in eliminating the tranquility
of the somnolent summer.

The Ghostly Parade

I watched as she paraded her ducklings
across the common, a proud mama,
her three babies trailing behind,
wobbling from side to side in their hurry
to keep up. Such darling creatures,
this new crop of fuzzy feathered
infants, learning the lessons of life
from their protective parent.

Every day the tiny troupe ventured out
into the newness of their world
led by their tolerant teacher, fondled
when obedient, scolded when not,
surveying cautiously the world
around them, sensing the fear
of foreboding predators that awaited
the instant of their distraction.

I looked forward each day to the parade
of this vulnerable family as they wandered
upon their predicted path to maturity,
nourishing, feathering, fluttering wings
in anticipation of flight. I watched
and possessively locked each duckling
into my heart as if it was my own.

Then one day, driving along the road
bordering the common, I suddenly
looked ahead and to my horror saw
the mother and her three ducklings
crossing the road directly in my path.
They stood frozen, staring into my eyes
as I bore down upon them. Too late
to avoid them, I slammed the brakes.

With hammering heart, I swerved
to the berm and looked behind. Nothing.
The road was empty. Where were they?
Surely I had killed them, impossible
they could have escaped. Leaving the car
I ran back to the scene. Not one feather
floated in the air. Not one smear of blood.

Had I dreamed this? While driving
had my concentration wandered and suddenly
awakening thought I saw them? Was it a mirage,
this vision springing before my eyes?
Had they existed only in my imagination?

I never saw them again parading the common,
so full of life, anticipating their unexplored future.
Had they just been ghosts parading in my thoughts?

Winter's Tears

They caress my eyes, my lips,
leaving their imprint
of purity upon my face.

Resembling freshly shed tears,
they trundle like iridescent pearls
down my stinging cheeks.

I taste their evasiveness
as they roll down to my mouth
and melt into the pretext of saliva,

as the Eucharist wafer
placed gently on the extended tongue
to be savored like Christ's body.

Winter is crying in remorse
for its crucifixion of summer,
its tears a purification of death.

Winter's Dark Journey

When winter begins
its darkened journey,
lowering the sun's
waning wick, I watch
as the patterns of light
move slowly across my wall,
disappearing from sight,
no longer filling my room
with warmth, no longer
wakening me
from drug-filled dreams
with a sense of elation.

How wondrous it would be
if I could fill a jar
with the sun's radiance,
seal the lid, place it on a shelf,
and when darkness steals
light from the sky,
open that precious jar
letting those captured rays
escape imprisonment
to expel the ghostly shadows
that hover in corners
filling my heart with dread.

Tin Men

Let's build ten thousand robots
To send off to the war,
And if they win the battles,
We'll build a million more.

We'll make them strong and mighty,
With titanium under-bolts.
They'll impassively march cross the land
Hurling ten million thunderbolts.

The enemy will counter
With fiery missiles through the sky,
But all their carnage has no strength:
Androids transmogrify.

No more we'll bury heroes
Who spill their sacred blood.
When tin men fall upon the ground,
They merely rust into the mud.

Let's build those raging robots
To replace our brave young men.
Only mad men dare to contemplate
The choice twixt flesh and tin

Who's Steering the Ship?

Who's steering the ship for this crazy world?
He's getting us dizzy; he's getting us whorled.
Who's up in the wheelhouse charting this route?
Whoever it is is keeping moot.

Where once we sailed waters calm and balmy,
We now plow through seas more like a tsunami.
Where is the captain who once kept us afloat?
Is the devil now gunning this crazy boat?

We're hitting tornadoes, we're rolled side to side,
Seeming more like a mad roller coaster ride.
Our hands keep sliding from the slippery rails,
The ship is floundering without any sails.

How can we not but be in a slough
Knowing that death is climbing the prow?
What has humanity to look forward to
When a boat with no rudder is going askew?

Oh, Captain, mad Captain, if we can't leave this ship
Without being wrapped in a black-body slip,
Then let us return to a more sturdy craft
Where winds were diminished to only a waft.

The Transition

When you wake, the images that linger
in your semi consciousness seem real:
refusing to evaporate into the recesses
of your dream-drugged world.

Your subconscious, wanting to retain
those visions that disappear with the sun,
battles against the light that scatters them
like wind dislodging cobwebs
hanging from hidden corners of darkness.

Slowly sleep retreats, thrusting you
into the harshness of reality,
wiping away those comforting illusions
you desperately want to cling to
before daylight sweeps them away.

With piercing eyes you search your mind,
hoping to rekindle the warmth
of that fading dream, but the sun's glare
bars your reentrance, forcing you
to retreat from that enviable twilight zone.

The Promise

I am the carpet you lovingly tread upon
in Spring whose tender tendrils cushion
your feet as you walk barefoot over me,
rejoicing in my ascension from winter's tomb.

As I shed the shackles of death,
my listless leaves gather strength,
pushing up through molting soil
to expose my face to warming sun,
filling my body with green plasma
nourishing the minutiae of life.

I am the protector of earth's terrain,
spreading my roots like fingers
entwining and knotting together each clod
into an intricately designed pattern,
creating a blanket of lush verdancy,
preserving the soil from erosion.

I am the alpha and omega of life.
I am the hope of eternal Spring,
keeping the promise to mankind
that there is eternity, even through death.

Reality

Don't dream of dreams unreachable.
Don't wish for feats unobtainable.
They cannot be interchangeable
So let them be transitional.

Be happy with the simple things,
For stress and worry always brings
Unhappiness. There are no gains
In flying with unstable wings.

Once Upon a Time

I loved so forcefully my heart shattered
into a thousand sharp-edged shards.
How can one live with a shattered heart?

Once upon a time I loved, but never again was I
to feel the pulsation of an overstimulated heart;
never again to hear my blood surging
into my ears like the pounding of waves
forced into the canals of those auricles;
never again to live with the expectation
of a love overwhelming my senses.

How can one dare be so rash
as to brave the casualty of another love
with a splintered heart pieced back together?

Gather Ye Rosebuds while Ye May
(A parody on Robert Herrick's poem)

Gather ye rosebuds while ye may,
For ye may stumble on your way,
And nary a rosebud can ye find
That blooms upon a climbing vine.

If ye doth find a thorny hedge
Where roses bloom, as so alleged,
Ye must acutely be aware
Not to pluck them with fingers bare.

If rosebuds ye doth hanker for,
Buy them from a flower store,
And if a thorn doth prick thy hand,
Ye then can sue them for a grand!

Reflected Images

Lying inertly on the bureau,
its mirrored glass is faded and stained
with age, its silver tarnished
by years of clasping fingers.

How many images have been reflected
within its glass? When new,
it must have given off visions
of youth, happy smiles, hope.

How many tears have fallen
on its surface; tears shed
from a reflection casting off warnings
of advancing age, oncoming death?

Hiding behind its discolored glass
are a thousand faces depicting
over the years the life of the beholder
who stared into its apathetic surface.

It was my mother's mirror
and her mother's before her.
Now it is mine, tarnished and stained,
never again to reflect youth.

Weariness

I've viewed it all before, you see:
The sun, the rain, the moon, the stars,
And in my future's fleeting hours,
There's little left in store for me.

I've seen the sun innumerable times
Arise, though more than often plagued
By clouds that rarely ever begged
Forgiveness for their injurious crimes.

I've felt the rain upon my face
That washed away my grievous tears;
Tears encrusted by the years
With sins I can no longer trace.

I've watched the moon glide through the sky,
Whose radiance obscured the night.
I've seen a thousand of its flights
And fathom not the reason why.

I've traced the myriad galaxies
But never memorized their names.
I know their brilliance never wanes,
Since they have weathered eternities.

Though there are things I've yet to see,
I care not whether they exist.
My weariness makes me desist
From caring what is yet to be.

The Tolling

There are bells ringing Sundays that declare amnesty
For those sinners who suffer devout apathy.
Then there are bells tolling out a glad overtone
Proclaiming to the world there's no cause to bemoan,
All is well, there's no threat to foresee.

When my ears are attuned to the toll of the bells,
I can soon comprehend if some sound therein dwells
That would justify fearing the message they bear,
Or if there is an omen that makes me despair
Of the toll that is my destiny.

When the clapper slams hard 'gainst the rim of the bell
And the pigeons soar up as if blown from hell,
Then I'll know what I've heard is the theme for my dirge
And the striker that's pounding with ominous urge
Is the death bell that's tolling for me.

The Silent Repentance

Today you died! The last day I was to hold you
in my arms as the morphine dripped slowly
into your veins, numbing your suffering body
to the unbearable pain tearing you apart.
As time ticked away, each beat of your heart waned.

> *Oh, my wife, I was too proud to tell you how much*
> *I loved you. I thought it would weaken my control*
> *over you, leaving holes in my flesh that would expose*
> *my weaknesses. All too late. I can no longer*
> *utter those words. They have choked me.*

My love, my love, let me lie beside you, warming
your cold skin with the warmth of my living flesh.
I remember the nights in our youth as we lay together,
our bodies aflame with desire. All I can give you now
are the dying embers of those memories.

> *What a good wife you were. Even when I*
> *forced my will upon you, you were not bitter.*
> *You understood how afraid I was to have my pride*
> *exposed as a cloak of insecurity. You protected me.*
> *You knew me for my weaknesses and loved me.*

Oh, my husband, how will I find the courage
to endure now you no longer are near me?
Why were you so afraid to speak of love?
I saw it in your eyes, in your touch.
But I wanted to hear you speak those words.

> *I die, never to tell you I loved you.*
> *I stifled it from fear you would find me weak*
> *and in reprisal devour my strength.*
> *How little I knew of strength! What consolation*
> *it would have given you. I die repentant!*

This I Tell You!

Listen to my voice from the grave!
You wrapped that rope around my neck,
cheering as you watched my body
swinging back and forth from the rafter.
But what did you accomplish?

I lie in my grave hearing the turmoil exploding
overhead. You toppled my statute, disbanded
my army, my police force, and left my country
in turmoil. You've brought about more killings
than occurred during my entire regime.

What fools you were thinking you
could conquer this land. You'll see it
torn apart, gaining nothing,
not even the oil you dreamed of possessing.

Now you'll see the Sunnis, the Shiites,
the Kurds killing each other to gain control.
Iraq will be torn apart, plundered by its neighbors
waiting to fill their coffers with our black gold.

You will rue the day you invaded Iraq
and sent me to the gallows. Islam proclaims
an eye for an eye and a tooth for a tooth.
This I tell you from my forsaken grave.

My Phoenix

Will I rise from my ashes when the flames
of cremation have consumed my flesh?
Will I soar in a golden blaze of resurrection
into the brilliance of a new and glorious day?

Phoenix, my Phoenix, my dream of eternal life,
are you but a myth taunting my doubting mind,
a symbol rising with the sun into an opiate heaven
only to plunge into the grave at night?

What Is Love?

"What is love?" I asked the sky.
"Love," it spoke in grave reply,
"Is the sun's attempt to scale my walls
And sit as king within my halls.
But with my yielding, I confess,
No one sees my emptiness."

"What is love?" I asked the sea.
And it answered with serenity:
"Love, my child, is ebb and tide.
But remember this," it softly sighed,
"That when it ebbs, suppress your fears.
Life goes on in spite of tears."

"What is love?" I asked the tree,
Who jovially cast its eyes on me.
"Love is like the birth of spring
When all my boughs are green again
And all my children come to nest.
For giving is love's happiness."

"What is love?" I asked the earth
And knew it words would be of worth.
"Love is sowing kindly seeds
Unmindful if your reaping's weeds.
It's planting deep within your soul
The thought that love's the final goal."

"What is love?" myself I asked
And pondered this prophetic task.
"Love is giving," said the tree;
"Ebbing always," spoke the sea.
At last I knew—then love must be
The secret of eternity.

Plea to Morpheus

Sleep, you have forsaken me!
You ignore all those sheep I've counted
until I have no more space to put them.
Then you pry open my eyes with thoughts
I dare not explore when I'm awake.

You force images into my brain
that circle round and round
finding no escape even though I try
replacing them with peaceful thoughts
to quiet me and bring tranquility.

Unable to arouse even the simplest visions,
I thrust my mind to my feet and inch by inch
imagine the calming flow of blood rising
higher and higher, hoping the sensation
of such peaceful relaxation will calm me.

Nothing can help! You've deserted me.
Craving your solace, I rise and, in desperation,
open that forbidden bottle of sleeping pills.
Just one night of peaceful sleep is all I ask.
How many will it take to bring oblivion?

Full Circle

If happiness is based upon our age,
how are we able to cross that bridge

from the protection of the cradle
to the dreaded anticipation of our death?

If only we could burn that effigy
that haunts us. But it seems so futile
when life is spent circling our grave.

The Illegal

He stands, leaning against the shadowed side
of WalMart small and thin, dressed in black
as if announcing doom. A lone figure
almost invisible because of his small stature,
except for the blaze in his eyes, as if daring
you to stare. He stoically waits for hire.

There is no doubt of his status: an immigrant
who crossed the border illegally, so desperate
for work he will wait for hours. How many
mouths has he to feed forcing him into this
humiliation? How many eyes have stared
causing him to shrink even smaller?

And yet he waits, shifting his slight weight
from foot to foot, trying to endure the degradation
of his position, fearful there will be no work,
fearful there will be no money to send to fill
those empty stomachs, fearful he may be caught.
And so he waits resignedly for hire.

The Oath

Toll the bells, blast off the cannons,
bow to the cheering crowds, smile
until your face wants to split
from the expansion of your lips.
This you do for pomp and circumstance.

Don't let your hand tremble as you place
it on the Bible to swear your oath
of office. Don't falter in your response
but keep your voice strong and sure.
It's all for pomp and circumstance.

Attend the luncheon in your honor.
Smile and acknowledge even those
who appear as strangers. Grasp their hands
in familiarity. It's the game of pretense,
and all for pomp and circumstance.

Appear at each of the many balls.
Greet the crowds joyously
as if this was your sole pleasure.
Dance with your wife with tired feet—
Just for pomp and circumstance.

All this pomposity could exhaust
a man even before he enters
the portals of the Oval Office.
Steady your hand as you hold that pen.
It's all for pomp and circumstance.

To the Sun God

Helios, Greek god of the sun, your flaming chariot
rises each day from the east out of the River Okeanos,
bearing you across the heavens with fiery energy and
down into the western land of the Hesperides.

You awaken Serene, goddess of the moon,
from the embrace of her princely shepherd lover,
making her soar through the heavens to keep the night sky
alight with the reflection of your imperious power.

Though we believe solely in one God, still we pray for you
to rise unendingly from your easterly throne to bring
us the joy of your eternal light and to bathe our bodies
in your baptismal fire, for without you nothing would exist.

Shining star, that brings the world out of darkness
into luminous light, it's wholly bewildering that mankind
no longer worships you as did the Greeks, for how
could we live without your body-nurturing light?

The House of Glass

It stands, a symbol of susceptibility, provoking
its neighbors into a desperate desire to smash
with fistfuls of rocks each sun-reflected pane
that forces its solar rays into their eyes,
enlarging the pupils as if with donnabella.

They want to throw those stones, but fearing
their action would expose their own guilt,
they lower their hands, regretfully dropping
the pebbles to earth, fearful the prediction
of *casting the first stone* would sear their souls.

Those stones, which personify their own sins,
cannot be thrown randomly since they themselves
live in glass houses, and those symbolic accusations
would be hurled back at them like a boomerang
homing in to shatter their transparent transgressions.

If you live in a house of glass, tear it down
and build your home from stone, free of censure,
letting no hypocrisy creep through the cracks,
for it will be voraciously decried by those
who zealously will your destruction.

A Letter to Spring

My Beloved Spring,

How longingly I wait for your return. Your absence
has left a chill within my heart that can be melted
only by the closeness of your clement body.
You left me with the covenant that Summer would
replace the sadness I would suffer from your loss,
but Summer failed to fill your glibly given promise.
Even Fall did not console me. He gave a month
of warmth, and then he sapped the colors from the trees
and seared the grass into a browned and withered corpse.
Then that dreaded child Winter came roaring in
with frigid claws and froze me with his vengeful snow.
I endured his frenzy knowing soon you would return.

My dearest Spring, I write to you with joy in knowing
soon I'll hold your tender body close to me,
gladly forgetting my other fickle children.

Your devoted and loving Mother Earth

Braving Spring

Ah, little green sprout,
I've caught you peeking
through the soil and peering
around to see if winter
has disappeared
before you pushed
your head and shoulders
up above the ground.

But is it wise of you
to be so venturesome?
What would you have done
if suddenly a winter wind
had caught you square
upon your curious, roving eyes?

Could you have hunched
yourself back down
into the thawing earth?
Or would the shock
of such a threat
have paralyzed retreat
to leave you frozen
in your quest?

I commend you for your valor,
little sprout. I touch your tiny
tendril head with a loving hand,
whispering sweet "ohs" and ahs,"
and hope my prayers
encourage you to brave
the fickleness of Spring.

Leaves

They lay on the ground, brittle and dry,
forced from their branches, no longer useful

to the tree that fed them the fluids of life.
At first, they appeared like black Grackles

that swarm in flocks and alight upon the ground
in search of worms, for they moved back and forth

as if alive, but when they did not take flight
I saw them for what they were: dead leaves,

fertilizer for the soil, mulch for the grass,
dancing the Dance Macabre in the wind.

The Sucklings

The ailing little lilac bush
braves the subnormal temperatures
of this vengeful spring
like a sorrowful mother
trying to nurse her children
with milk-less breasts.

The tiny leaves force themselves
out upon the branches striving
to live, sucking the insufficient
fluids from her limbs,
teething on the dry branches,
relentless of her weakness.

Will she survive another winter
when her roots no longer
can absorb earth's nutrients?
Will she bring forth more children
that suck away her life
leaving her barren and brittle?

Poor little lilac bush,
once bearing beautiful children
growing up with festive
lavender gowns flowing
with the summer breezes;
you gave your life for them.

The Tower of Silence

In Bombay, I stood and stared up at that
oppressive structure looming on the horizon.
What a foreboding sight that Tower of Silence,
the religious ritual for the Parsi dead,
the funeral pyre for scavenging vultures
to gorge upon decaying flesh.

They blacken the sky with their presence
when they see from afar a funeral procession
approaching. Their beating wings fill the air
with a sinister sound. With undeterred concentration
they circle, awaiting the sacrificial food . . .

When only ossein is left, their gluttonous shrieks
for the spoils and the ominous sound
of their beating wings have quieted,
an eerie silence fills the air. The vultures
have finished their meal and the bones are left
to calcify upon that formidable Tower of Silence.

That Old Stainin' Tree
(Parody on James Whitcomb Riley's "The Mulberry Tree")

My dear Mr. Riley, that mulberry tree
You so fondly describe as a dear memory
Seems a bit overstated and dimmed by those years
That elapsed since your childhood, and now it appears
As a picture once savored without much detail
Of how those mulberries, so juicy and hale,
Did plunk to the ground in precarious clumps
Awaiting to sully young boys' feet and rumps.

So today as you dream of that mulberry tree
With its wide spreadin' limbs all shakin' so free
And spreadin' around all those berries so mauled
Upon the terrain whare the pastur' was bald,
Was there nothin' astirrin', no mem'ries concrete
Of the stain from those berries upon your bare feet?
Perhaps all those years spent away from that scene
Have dimmed your retention and washed your feet clean.

The Timing of the Snail

The rabbit and the snail one day
Decided they would race.
Of course, the rabbit knew he'd win,
Knowing well the snail's slow pace.

They set a date and spread the news,
Inviting all the local creatures
Who sat in total wonderment
Upon their grassy bleachers.

The starting point was at the well
Then race down to the spot
Which they had chosen as the end—
A mere ten yards they sought.

The reason for this shorter length
Was the rabbit's sly injection.
He knew the snail would move so slow
He'd utter no objection.

And well he knew, this sneaky hare,
With such a short expanse,
He'd reach the end before the snail
Could even have a chance.

The starting bell was loudly made
By a beaver as the judge
Who smacked his tail against the well
That gave the two a nudge.

So off they went, the two of them
With the viewers loudly cheering.
The rabbit gave a mighty leap
While the snail seemed barely gearing.

The little mollusk tried his best,
For he knew he had no time,
So he raised his tail as he slid along
To leave a trail of slime.

By now the rabbit reached the goal
And turned to view his rival
Who seemed so very far behind
He doubted his arrival.

The thought of waiting at the goal
Seemed endless to the hare,
So he bounded back along the path
To give the snail a scare.

Now a snail is blind and cannot see,
He can only smell a prey,
So when his rival reached his side,
He let his mucus splay.

The rabbit stepped into the slime
And from habit licked his feet,
Not knowing to ingest this thing
Would make his bowels secrete.

Alas, alack, the rabbit groaned
With dreadful stomach pain.
He rolled upon the grassy path
And felt his power drain.

He watched in dreaded agony
As the mollusk glided on,
Knowing well his hopeful thoughts
Of victory were gone.

And so the snail in his own time
Reached that envious goal post.
By outwitting that audacious hare
He now had cause to boast.

The moral of this witless tale
Is beware of whom you dare,
For if you think you'll win the race,
You're an addle-minded hare.

Limericks

There was a young fellow named Brinker
Who thought that all gardening a stinker.
He said posies were "rot"
And instead planted pot . . .
But the cops dragged him off to the clinker

A lady named Valery Bunker
Resolved in the shower she'd hunker.
But when May came around
She couldn't be found,
For her showers in April had shrunk her

In April '04, the newscasters said,
"The Capitol's water was full of lead."
So now we all know
Why the Legislature's so slow—
It all settled into its head!

"I slept like a baby," he happily said
As he woke from a sleep of the dead.
His remark was allegoric
And precisely rhetoric,
For he discovered he'd wet in the bed!

Haiku

surging black-hued clouds
furrow the sky with anger
planting seeds of rain

raindrops dance on pond
turning its tranquil surface
into bubbling stew

Christmas Day dinner
overabundance of food
jingle belly ache

Christmas carolers
turn ozone to vapored frost
notes frozen in flight

New Year's Eve galas
drinking to incoming year
whoopee brings headache

Beware of Your Prayers

We needed rain. We prayed to end the drought,
and maybe some even did a rain dance,
hoping a few pounding drum beats
would stir the atmosphere into motion.

We prayed until we ran out of beseechments
and the rain dancers danced until their legs ached,
but the sky refused to open its flood gates.
The soil crusted and began to fissure.

The grass shriveled from the merciless sun.
The flowers drooped, seeming to await
the last sacrament. The creek beds
bared their nakedness in shame.

Suddenly, in response to our prayers
and the frantic beating of drums, scowling
rain clouds swirled across the heavens
pounding the earth with their watery wrath,

flooding creek beds, soaking the soil with unrelenting
anger, causing saturation that could only rise.
Lord of the Universe, we prayed for rain, but
did you have to answer so intensely our prayers?

In the Attic of My Mind

I have stored all those memories in little boxes,
now covered with dust, in the attic of my mind,
where they bear labels of love, despair, sorrow,
and regret; so small the box for contentment.

I mount the stairs to that attic with reluctance.
The climb is painful, my feet stumbling on every step.
When I force open the door to that secreted room,
hidden memories of the past swirl about my head

like a dust storm in the arid plains, blinding me
to the clarity of the peace that fills my life today.
My fingers tremble as I unlock each box to release
those memories that have been so carefully hidden.

Why do I hoard them still? They no longer
share the present. They are a cancer
that should be cut out with a knife and let to bleed
until the last palpitation ensures their death.

If only I had the strength to release them.
If only I could open that attic window
and throw them out like bloated moths
forced from their devastation.

The Seduction of the Wind-

The wind surges through the trees
whipping their branches round and round
in a mad capricious dance, grasping
and bending them to the ground.
The leaves swirl and twirl, twisting
back and forth as if maddened
by the effects of Ecstasy.

They have no choice but to submit
to the wind, succumbing to its virility,
seduced by its strength like an aroused
woman powerless to reject
the overpowering advances
of her insistent lover, surrendering
to the throbs of the wind's passion

Ode To My Coffee Mug

O mug, whose lip I grant to touch my own,
Your contents rouse the fibers of my mind
And put to flight those dreams my sleep has sown.

You are my morning joy when I arise;
Your essence stronger than a lover's arms
Does make my dreaming mind to fantasize.

To feel your warmth within my circled hand
When filled with aromatic coffee blends,
You give me strength to truthfully withstand

The dark uncertainties that may attack.
You are my joyous morning metaphor,
My anticipated aphrodisiac.

What would I do if you rebuffed my touch
And in defiance to my love for you
Did fling yourself in suicidal grutch

Upon the floor as Humpty-Dumpty fell
From off the wall and no King's men could put
His splattered innards back into his shell?

Dear mug, I beg you not to take that path,
For then how could I stimulate my mind
To free myself from slumber's aftermath?

O mug, you are not as Keat's Grecian urn
Which is so unapproachably taciturn.

My Little Poetry Book

Are you collecting dust upon that shelf,
my little book? Has no one run a finger
down your spine in curiosity?
Has anyone dislodged you from between

the confines of those large imposing volumes
squeezing you into oblivion?
You sit upon that shelf so disregarded
by the world I now regret your birth.

Will you forgive my lonely words in which
I bared my soul? I meant no injury.
I wanted only to release the pain
that tore away my heart with anguished love.

So now, my little book, it's only you
and I who sit abandoned on our shelves,
just you and I whose covers gather dust
upon the pages of our lonely hearts.

At Sunset

When the sinking sun reclines
its weary head upon horizon's breast
and the blood-red sky closes its eyes
against the oppressive strain
of an arduous day;
when the darkened drapes of night
are drawn across earth's stage
preparing for the closure of day,
then I too fold my tent,
as the Bedouins, and leave behind
the disquietudes of a demanding day.

Fame

(Rondel)

I pound, I pound, why aren't you there?
   Why can't you hear my pounding fist?
   There is no way I can desist
From pounding 'til you're made aware
My anxious heart is in despair
   And that is why I must persist.
I pound, I pound, why aren't you there?
   Why can't you hear my pounding fist?

I promise not to scowl or glare
   If you declare I don't exist.
   I'll turn away and not persist.
But oh, my heart is in despair!
I pound, I pound, why aren't you there?

My Father Wore Trojans

When I was a child I remember one day
snooping through my parents' bureau drawers.
I had no business there, but curiosity was one
of my weaknesses. While rummaging through
one drawer, I discovered a little red tin box
with the head of a man wearing a strange helmet.

I held it in my hand and worked laboriously
to pry open the lid. Inside were these small
wide-necked balloons. Wow! Were they
to be a gift to us girls or just hidden away
to be blown up for the Fourth of July? I tried
to blow one up but had not the breath to fill it.

My curiosity sated, I placed it back in the box,
closed the lid, shut the drawer, and forgot
the incident . . . that is until one day while trying
to grope for something that had fallen
under their bed, I had to crawl on my back
to reach whatever it was that had rolled there.

And then I saw them: those little wide-necked
balloons! There they were stuffed between
the mattress and the springs. Dozens of them,
all dried up, brittle to the touch and looking
very depleted. Why would my parents blow
them up and stuff them under the mattress?

As I grew older and learned the purpose
of those little balloons I couldn't blow up,
one memory kept flooding my mind:
the memory of their bed so often crashing
to the floor. Those little balloons stuffed between
the mattress and the bed springs were the cause.

Ballad For Terri Winchell
(Who was viciously murdered in 1981)

He wrapped a belt around her neck and strained
until it broke and then, with hammer, crushed
her skull with twenty-three vicious strokes.
But still unsatisfied, he dragged her bleeding body
from the car and raped her inert form and then,
to verify her death, stabbed her twenty times.

Why must we pity Michael Morales who
without compassion murdered Terri Winchell?
Should we, as Christ upon the cross, cry out,
Forgive them, for they know not what they do?
But he knew what he did!

Now there are those who walked from San Francisco
all the way to San Quentin Prison for abolition
of his punishment, bearing signs to nullify
his execution, saying it's cruel and stupefying
punishment to put to death a man with lethal shots
of chemicals that take up to seven minutes to die.

How long did he prolong the life of Terri Winchell
as he tortured her? What injustice must we tolerate
when mercy for the murderer is greater than
that given to the victim, when tears are shed
from senseless eyes and hearts no longer feel
the pain inflicted by the evil in this world?

I sing a ballad of the death of Terri Winchell.

Beware the Piper

Covered with the glitter and glamour of a prostitute
promoting her wares, she lured the pleasure seekers
into her streets of frenzied jazz, sensuous foods,
houses of iniquitous delights, with endless nights
and sunlit days unseen, except through the slats
of the closed shutters where light dared to penetrate.

She defied fate to meddle in her provocative ways,
challenged the gods to interfere in her voracious desire
for worldly pleasures, ignored the rumors of impending
doom that hung over her like the reaper's robe,
and was so impregnated with gluttony and lust
she forgot the Piper who was waiting for his pay.

But the Piper growing tired of her mounting debts,
demanding payment in full, hurled the winds
of destruction down upon her, tore her frivolous
façade to shreds, broke through her pretentious levy,
transformed her gaudy streets into canals of stench
that oozed from the bowels of her over-indulged sewers.

The innocent died while the devourers of her flesh
fled, taking with them their insatiable appetites
to feed upon another beckoning strumpet who promised
all those pleasures that Katrina stole from them
in their beloved pleasure-filled harlot, New Orleans.
Beware of the Piper who waits to collect his dues!

Of What Consequence?

I ask myself, who were those predecessors
who preceded me: those earth-plodding
ancestors whose genes I carry
in my blood? Have I a likeness to that
first hereditary gene that persevered
through life with little consequence?

I

My mother's father, a transit tenant farmer,
overburdened the muck-layered earth with onions.
He sired seven daughters who were forced
to toil in the onion fields along with him
with little to show for their labors.
It's said he drank up all the profits—perhaps
to wash the stench of onions from his guts.

I no longer recall my mother's father,
who died when I was just a little girl.
Yet I am part of him as much as he
was part of his forefathers. This man,
of whom I have but one vague memory—
a time when sitting on his lap he sang—
lived, and yet I don't recall his song.

II

My mother's mother bore the drudgery
of child bearing, planting onions, and moving
from farm to farm because they were too poor
to own their land. It's said her family
had means. And for this man, she sacrificed
her life to stain her hands with onions? The marriage
bed's elusive, but because of that, I am.

When her husband died, she had no home,
moving from daughter to daughter,
intruding upon their lives for those brief months.
She coughed and spat her life away with asthma.
She died in the house of my grandparents,
a house where she was not welcomed
by my father's mother. Was that a life to celebrate?

III

For my paternal grandmother, I have
little memory; she died when I was young.
I should remember more, but it's as if
the camera had no film. A small determined
woman, she ruled her home in the righteousness
of God, yet condemned the presence of
my mother's mother living in her house!

She bore ten children, all raised with the fear of God
in their hearts, but interjected pain in my mother's!
It's said I have her eyes, but that I dispute.
I felt no love for her, for when she died,
I was tearless when I should have wept. I didn't
know then my mother was freed from her oppressor.
My mother suffered the consequence of that!

IV

My father's father was old when I was born.
He built his home, farmed his land, held tight
to the profits he made, and ruled his world
with an iron hand. How proud I was when I saw
his name on the school's plaque as one of its founders.
I rejoiced that I was a part of him,
and yet I trembled under his rigid gaze.

He let me count his money. How exciting
it was to feel the coins in my hands, and how
reluctant I was to have to give them back.
He lived his life: sneaked a swig of whiskey
when grandmother was not around, smoked
a pipe, and never went to church—a letdown
to his wife. He was a man of the earth.

V

My father was the youngest of their children.
He was pampered by his mother and bent
to the wishes of his folks to take control
of his father's farm, but when his parents died,
he sold the farm and moved the family
to town where finally he was able to break
away from the bonds of his dependency.

A small man, he didn't inherit the ambitions
of his father but reaped the voice of his mother.
He sang away his worries and charmed my mother
into his arms, but all his life he labored
to pay my mother's medical bills. Loved by all,
he believed in the adage of "speak no evil"
and amassed no money. He was the common man.

VI

My mother was the result of the onion fields.
One of seven siblings, she was forced
to toil in the fields beside them. With a drinking
father and a tired mother, she strived to get free,
and when, at seventeen, she met my father,
he planted his seed within her. A forced marriage
displeased his mother, and there began the tale.

She was a tiny soul who lacked self-esteem
and was cowered by her husband's mother.
Enduring the pressure of having to live with in-laws
and a husband too weak to support her will,
she suffered depression all her life. I knew her suffering,
but only in maturity did I understand:
A despondent woman, a desolated life.

VII

And I? What have I accomplished,
of what consequence am I? Those kinsmen
before me, what did they accomplish? Did they,
as I, question the value of their lives? How minute
we are, how insignificant our lives seem to appear
in the overall scheme of perpetuity:
A few dry bones that disintegrate into dust.